GENERATIONAL WEALTH

GENERATIONAL WEALTH

Khaleel Riyaadh Siddiq

J. Kenkade
PUBLISHING

Bryant, Arkansas

J. Kenkade Publishing
5920 Highway 5 N. Ste. 7
Bryant, AR 72022
www.jkenkadepublishing.com
Social Media: @jkenkadepublishing

J. Kenkade Publishing is a registered trademark.

Printed in the United States of America

This book is dedicated to the youth.
Let your light shine so that you can navigate
yourself out of darkness and into the light.
I wish I could do more for you but at this
time this book is all I can do and is my
way of me doing something to bring about
balance for the ones without it who come
in to contact with my message of peace,

positivity and prosperity.

-Khaleel

*Author of "Positive Quotes", Mind Over
Matter", "Hope", and "Generational Wealth"*

❧

I'm not writing this book because I think I'm better than you or because I'm a person outside of the box who doesn't have to worry about the struggles within that many are enduring. I'm writing this book because I empathize with you and because I care... I truly do. I hope my words bring life, light, and visibility into your important life.

❧

❧

Why sacrifice your mental weapon for a physical one that will only take you so far? Or take you to a land that's not meant for you to dwell in by nature, a land that advocates for the most part rising through different levels of darkness, in many ways.

❧

❧

Why rise through different levels of darkness when you have the ability, the power, to rise through different levels of light?

❧

❧

To the young reading this book, don't throw your life away or sacrifice your freedom trying to accomplish a quick success. There are many possible ways you can accomplish that same success with patience, perseverance, and righteousness.

❧

❧

Don't give up, be patient, be wise, and be the best you. You are still young with a whole future ahead of you, so protect it and embrace it.

❧

❧

If you don't make the right choices now, later on in life you will be effected- life will be more difficult. You will be effected because life will be more difficult to navigate. You will be effected because life will be more difficult to manage.

❧

❧

Don't go out bad trying to paint a picture that has been painted by many painters before you. Paint a new one! You have the power in your mind to do so! You are equipped with all the tools you need. You have a choice to utilize those tools, or to set them to the side to collect dust and use the tools of the world that you think help you get somewhere but in reality, gets you nowhere.

❧

Don't throw your life away-you only have one. You might gamble and win but sooner or later you will gamble and loose. That's just the nature of the dice game. My advice from me to you is to not gamble at all. Stay away from those casino type environments and get rid of the gambling spirit and casino type of mind.

❧

You are loved by people you don't even know love you. The question is, do you love yourself? Do you really love yourself? Oh, you do? Then let it be shown. Let it be known. Get a career trade or degree and be the best that you can. I know you can do it and I'm hoping and praying for the day you start doing just that.

❦

❧

Don't sell dope of any kind. You might last a year, you might last five, but after so long it won't last any longer. It's just quick money for long term hardships/adversity, court dates, jail time, and the possibility of death. You have your whole life ahead of you. Why sacrifice that for a temporary high/status? Have you heard the quote, "There's more than one way to skin a cat?"

❧

❖

Crime doesn't pay, so don't work for it. There are no real healthy benefits. It is like cashing a check that will bounce sooner or later.

❖

❖

I hope that all the youngsters that are reading this book right now stop what they're doing if it's wrong and start doing what's right for the sake of their mind, spirit, and future.

❖

❦

Don't incarcerate yourself in this world only to be incarcerated in another. Break the cycle, my young brothers and sisters. You must break the cycle. I know you can do it, so if nobody else believes in you just know that I do.

❦

You will not like being told when to eat and when to take a shower being incarcerated with 30+ people in a cell block with minimum to zero freedom. How will you, the youth, be our future that the world needs for world reform, for the greater good, if you are incarcerated?

❧

There is more than one way to skin a cat, so why think you have no other options when you have many to choose from that are more healthy and rewarding?

❧

❧

Having a class one mindset doesn't exempt you from class four things in life, but it allows you to get through them with an unbreakable confidence to succeed, making you the successor at the end of the day.

❧

If right now you open the palm of your hand, you will see the world. That is power… will you waste it or put that power to use in the best of ways?

❧

The system has a job to do. It's up
to you and up to us to work for it or
work against it. We can either play
ball in our own backyards or play in
backyards filled with endless evils,
adversity, and consequences.

❧

❧

Walking on water is not just a phrase,
it is a way of life for those like you,
the youth. To be able to do just that,
you must believe and never let go
of that faith. Don't let your current
condition or evils of the world take
that from you.

❧

From Manuscript
to Masterpiece

Our Services
Author Retains Royalties & Rights

100% Royalties
Professional Proofreading
Copyright Registration
Online Self-Publishing Classes

For inquiries:
Website: www.jkenkadepublishing.com
Email: info@jkenkadepublishing.com

Also Available from
The Author and Publisher

ISBN: 978-1955186452
Visit www.amazon.com
Author: Khaleel Siddiq

Mind over Matter is the sequel to the author's first book, "Positive Quotes". It is filled with wisdom and words of inspiration from the author himself.

Also Available from
The Author and Publisher

ISBN: 978-1955186278
Visit www.amazon.com
Author: Khaleel Siddiq

This book is not just a book but is a book containing a key that if obtained through wisdom and understanding and by applying and believing in oneself to the utmost that one can believe, one can use this key to open doors that are not electronically monitored. This key is the most powerful weapon one can possess. This key is our mind. The author believes that our faith must be bigger than adversity. If not, then how can we overcome it? The author believes that life will teach us two things: strength and weakness.

Also Available from
The Author and Publisher

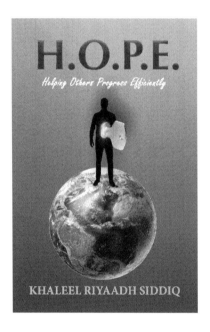

ISBN: 978-1955186520
Visit www.amazon.com
Author: Khaleel Siddiq

Our faith must be bigger than our barriers our faith must be greater than adversity if not we will only have ideas about success but not just any success but the success that we see for ourselves as individuals.

Made in the USA
Columbia, SC
05 August 2024